Tickletoe Tree Poetry

By Russ Towne

Tickletoe Tree Poetry
Copyright © 2016 Russ Towne

First Edition, April 2016

Russ Towne Publishing
Campbell, CA

Editing: Shayla Eaton, CuriouserEditing.com
Layout and Cover Design: Gail Nelson, e-book-design.com
Illustrations: Josh McGill and Christina Cartwright

ISBN 978-0-692-70460-8

1. Children's Fiction
2. Animals
3. Stories in Rhyme

To Earl and Nancy Shackelford
whose love and friendship I count
among my greatest blessings.

Table of Contents

V. G. and Dexter Dufflebee

My name is Dexter Dufflebee.
I love to travel to the sea.
Once when I was near a shore
I'd always wanted to explore,
I began to watch a butterfly
Flutter by in the sky.
I tripped on a rock I didn't see there
And gave myself a scary scare
When I fell into a prickly bush
With thorns so sharp, they hurt my tush!
I wriggled and scriggled but got more stuck.
I was in trouble and had run out of luck.
I took a big breath and started to shout,
"Someone please come and help me get out!"
I yelled until I could yell no more.
My poor voice box was really sore.
It hurt so much I could barely speak;
My shout became a tiny squeak.

Then I saw a little guy.

He proudly looked me in the eye

And said, "There's no need to fear.

Help is here. I'll get you clear."

From the top of his head

To the tip of his toes,

He was slightly less large

Than the size of my nose!

I said, "I'm too big and you're too small.

It's clear you have no chance at all."

He said, "I'll get you out, no need to worry.

You have the word of V. G. Mugurry."

I sneered, "You're no bigger than my ear!

I'll be stuck forever and left right here."

He replied, "You have nothing to lose to let me try.

I have big ideas for a little guy."

"Besides," he said in his little voice,

"It seems to me you have no choice.

So why not just wait and see

If I'm able to set you free."

"Okay," I sighed to V. G. Mugurry.

"I'll give you a chance, but please do hurry!

I'm tired of being in this bush,

These thorns are sharp and hurt my tush!"

Then he left, and I began to doubt

If he'd come back and get me out.

He returned with a wagon

So full it was saggin'.

V. G. replied, "I know I'm the only one,

But I can still get the job done.

I may be way too tiny to you,

But wait to see what I can do."

"I'll get you out, and not just try;

I have big ideas for a little guy.

I know this job is really tough,

But I brought with me all kinds of stuff.

Wood, rope, nails, and a hammer too.

I even brought a saw for you.

We'll get you out, just wait and see.

It won't be long before you're free."

V. G. was not the kind to shirk.

He grabbed his tools and went right to work.

V. G. lashed three ladders from rope and wood.

The knots he used were really good.

He leaned two ladders against the bush

And took great care to miss my tush.

Then, what did that little guy do?

He tied ladder three to the other two.

I didn't understand his plan at all.

And, he was so small, I feared he'd fall.

Then he screwed on a winch

And lowered two ropes inch by inch.

He yelled, "Tie these together under your tush.

We'll soon have you out of that prickly bush."

V. G. tied the rope to the winch,

Then yanked a crank and it moved an inch.

V. G. pushed with all his might,

But I was stuck mighty tight.

I feared the ladders would begin to break.

How much more stress could they take?

Then, very much to my surprise,

The ropes and I began to rise.

V. G. gave it all he had.

He was mighty strong for a tiny lad.

He pulled free and swung me around,

Then lowered me to the ground.

"Thank you! Thank you," I told V. G.

"You kept your word and rescued me."

"Though I am big and very tall,

And you are very, very small,

You were big enough to set me free.

You'll always have a friend in me.

You did what you said you'd do.

I never should have doubted you!

Will you walk with me to the shore?

We'll talk and see things to explore."

He said, "That sounds like lots of fun.

Yes, my friend, I'd love to come."

The Grumpadinkles

On a bright sunny day
with just one cloud in the sky
Grumbly Grumpadinkle asked with a sigh,
"Why won't the clouds just go away?
It looks like bad weather is here to stay."
His wife Gruffina glumly agreed.
That little cloud was all they'd need
To have it ruin their whole day.
They never had good things to say.
It was just the Grumpadinkle way.
That is, until today.
They heard a soft knock on the door.
"Who's disturbing me?" Grumbly asked in a roar.
"Why are they here? Why bother us?"
Grumbly grumbled and made a big fuss.

When he yanked open the door,
on his face was a scowl.
He asked, "What do you want?"
in a low Grumbly growl.
A little girl stood looking up,
And in her arms, she held a pup.
"I'm Wendy," she said.
"We just moved next door."
Gruffina grumbled,
"So that's why we've never seen you before."
The Grumpadinkles just stood there and stared.
This made Wendy a little scared.
But she never, ever lost her smile.
Then she asked in a little while,
"Would you please watch my pup today?
I have my allowance and I can pay.
My mommy's sick and daddy's away."
Mommy needs my help. Can my puppy stay?
His name is Hugger, and he plays all day."

Grumbly growled, "I might be allergic.

He might make me sneeze."

Wendy said, "Maybe you could hold him, please?"

Gruffina grouched, "He might have fleas

Or make a mess on the floor.

We've never had a dog before.

It sounds like he could be a chore."

Wendy looked about to cry.

Gruffina groaned and said with a sigh,

"We'll take your mutt since your mommy's sickly,

But we expect you to come back quickly."

Grumbly grumped,

"Give him to me before I change my mind."

Wendy smiled and said,

"Thank you for being so kind."

When the little girl left,

Grumbly grouched, "Now what do we do?"

Gruffina grumped, "I haven't a clue."

Trouble soon started when Grumbly put Hugger down.

The playful pup ran all around.

He sniffed, scratched, and raced all over their place.

He pulled on their curtains until they crashed down,

Knocking over a vase that was shaped like a clown.

He hopped on their bed and jumped all around,

Tearing open two pillows filled with goose down.

Feathers flew from here to there.

Feathers flew everywhere!

They saw all the damage and began to feel sick.

They tried to catch him, but he was too quick.

"He's headed for the kitchen," Grumbly growled, but too late.

Hugger knocked over a table set with good plates.

They clattered and shattered all over the floor.

He pulled milk and eggs from a fridge door

And two dozen spoons from a big drawer.

It all mixed together in a mess on the floor!

There were so many messes; there were messes galore!

Too many messes for them to ignore.

Grumbly tried to grab him but missed him instead.

He slipped on some water and fell on his head.

While he lay quite dazed on the floor,

With a bumped head that was really sore,

The pup dumped white flour on the clothes Grumbly wore!

He found pots and pans behind a door.

He banged and clanged them, then banged them some more.

Hugger tugged on an apron so hard that it tore.

The pup never tired and kept trying to explore.

They looked at the mess that had once been their place,

Then looked at the big smile on Hugger's face.

They saw a twinkle in his eyes,

And very much to their surprise,

They didn't feel mad.

They didn't feel sad.

Why, they almost felt glad!

Despite the great big mess they had.

Then they were surprised even more

When, in place of the frowns that they always wore,

A grin started growing, and after a while,

It got so big it became a smile.

The Grumpadinkles began to feel strange.

Something inside them started to change.

Grumbly said, "The thing that I'm feeling, I think it's called fun."

And it became clear the pup still wasn't done.

He danced on the counter and pranced with a wiggle.

That's when Gruffina started to giggle.

Soon she snickered and snorted, then even guffawed!

Then Grumbly chortled and chuckled! It all felt so odd!

When the Grumpadinkles began to laugh out loud,

Happy Hugger became mighty proud.

They laughed so hard they rolled on the floor.

They picked themselves up and laughed even more!

They laughed like they'd never laughed before!

That's when they heard a soft knock on the door.

Grumbly answered it with a great big grin.

"Hi, Wendy. Won't you please come in?"

Little Wendy looked all around.

Everything was turned upside down,

And that included the Grumpadinkles' frowns!

Hugger had in just a little while

Turned their sad frowns into great big smiles!

Wendy said, "My mommy's not sick anymore,"

As she picked her pup up off the floor.

Gruffina replied, "I'm glad your mommy feels better, dear.

Thank you for leaving Hugger here.

Please bring your pup another day.

We'd love another chance to play."

When Wendy said good-bye,

Grumbly glanced into the sky.

The day was bright and sunny with just one cloud.

He saw it and laughed out loud.

"I now see things in a better way.

It looks to me like a beautiful day."

Zach and the Toad Who Road a Bull

Zach's friends had frogs to jump and race.

They held contests all over the place

To see how far they'd jump and go.

They really put on quite a show.

Zach wanted a frog so he could play

With the other boys and their frogs all day.

He looked for hours without finding a frog

But then he spotted a toad on a log.

It had zebra-type stripes,

But instead of being black and white,

His stripes were purple and yellow.

He certainly was a colorful fellow.

The toad had a friendly face,

So Zach took him to a jump-and-race.

The other boys laughed but didn't mind

When Zach put his toad on the starting line.

He whispered, "Please try to jump far.

It's now your turn to be a star."

When the toad began to jump

The wind bumped him with a whump.

It caught the toad and pushed him back,

So far back the boys told Zach,

"No fair! Your toad doesn't score.

We won't play with him anymore!"

Zach whispered to his toad, "You're no slacker.

You jumped backward—I'll name you Backer.

I like you just the way you are!

To me you'll always be a star."

"If you want to stay with me

We'll be friends, just wait and see."

One day they went to a rodeo

To help Backer see the show.

Zach put him on a wooden rail,

But he was slapped by a horse's tail.

That pushed Backer so far back

He landed in a lady's lap!

She shrieked, "EEEK! What's that?"
And threw him onto a cowboy's hat.
Things were now very rough.
The rider who wore it looked mighty tough.
He didn't know Backer was on his head.
The announcer pointed to him and said,
"He'll be riding Last Ride Red."
The other wranglers all looked down,
For Last Ride Red was the meanest around.
No one rode him more than a second or two,
And when they hit the ground, they were black and blue.
That's when the announcer said,
"The reason he's called Last Ride Red
Is because every rider who's ever tried
Never, ever took another bull ride."
But this cowboy was mighty brave.
He would try to ride him anyway.

He climbed on the side of the big bull's pen,
Then leaned forward to look at him.
That's when Backer slid off the rider's hat,
Onto Last Ride Red's great big back!
That startled the man holding the gate.
He tried to close it but was too late.
Last Ride Red came charging out,
The crowd saw Backer and began to shout:
"That toad's in trouble! Everyone look out!"
Backer knew he had to hang on tight,
So he grabbed the bull's hair with all his might.
He knew for certain if he was thrown down,
He'd soon be stomped into the ground.
Last Ride Red was having a fit.
He ran through a fence, shattering it.
The bull jumped and leapt and even hopped.
He kept it up and never stopped.

His anger turned to a mighty rage
As he raced around that dusty stage.
But no matter how high and hard he bucked,
That brave little toad never gave up.
Red's hooves pounded all over the dirt.
Backer's bones and muscles really hurt.
The bull even tried leaping so high
His horns seemed to scrape the sky.
He jerked back and forth so quickly
Backer started feeling a little sickly.
Red romped and pounded and even snorted,
But little Backer was never thwarted.
After an hour of stomping all around,
Last Ride Red gave up and lay down.
Everyone jumped to their feet and cheered.
The bull hadn't done what they all feared.
Instead of the toad being stomped in the ground,
Backer rode the bull all the way down.

Zach ran out and picked Backer up,

Then a man gave them a buckle and trophy cup.

He yelled, "Congratulations, son!

Your brave little toad has really won!

No one's ever done

What he's done.

The best bull rider is right here.

Backer's our Rodeo Champ this year!"

The next day the news was full

Of how Backer the toad rode the great big bull.

The rodeo retired Last Ride Red.

He's a happy bull and very well fed.

He gets to eat grass and hay all day

And stay in a field full of cows and play.

His pasture's now longer and wider.

And though Backer was Last Ride Red's last rider,

Zach and Backer were Red's first friends

And this is how my poem ends.

Misty Zebracorn

My friend's a zebra with a great big horn.

Misty calls herself a Zebracorn.

When we went to a beach, she caused quite a scene

When she stayed in the sun without sunscreen.

Bad sunburn turned her white stripes red

From the tip of her tail to the hair on her head.

When we went for a swim, all her stripes washed off.

Some folks laughed at her. One started to scoff:

"Why, you're just a horse with a horn!"

I said, "This magical mare is a unicorn!"

For a moment, no one said a word.

I wasn't even sure they'd heard.

But in a little while, they began to smile.

"A unicorn!" we heard some say.

"Today is our lucky day!"

They stayed with us and splashed and played.

Pretty soon her stripes came back,

First black and red, then white and black.

I said, "Surely you are all aware that Misty Zebracorn

Is the luckiest unicorn that's ever been born."

Since that time we've all been friends,

And this is how my story ends.

Clyde and I

I went to say hi to new neighbors next door
And saw something I'd never seen before.
When I say what I saw, I hope you don't laugh
Because what I saw was a green giraffe.
He stood on his head out in the rain;
The poor wet guy was in a lot of pain.
His great green body swayed way up high,
His long lean legs stuck straight up in the sky.
I stood there staring at the startling view
As he ate a banana that was bright blue.
I've seen yellow bananas, and green ones too,
Even brown and black ones, but never blue.
I offered my red and white umbrella
To that half-drowned, upside-down fella.
He gratefully replied, "Hi, my name is Clyde.
Thanks for your kindness," the big guy cried.

And with a real long sigh, he said, "Silly me.
I untied a knot in a Tickletoe Tree.
Now what a pain in the neck I've got.
When I bend it wrong, it hurts a LOT.
I'm standing on my head to work out kinks,"
He painfully explained between raindrop blinks.
"I eat bananas to keep up my strength.
It takes lots of muscles for a neck this length."
Then he thought for quite a while
And on his face grew a great big smile.
"Would you please use my neck for a slide?
You'll help my muscles if you take a ride.
We'll make it a game and make it real fun.
If we're having fun, we've already won."
I knew right then we'd become good friends!
And this is how my happy story ends.

Clyde and I Help a Hippo to Fly

Clyde and I slurped Burzleberry Tea
As we laid in the shade of a Tickletoe Tree,
Its feathery leaves swayed in the breeze,
Tickling my toes and Clyde's knobby knees.
We giggled and laughed like best friends do,
Rolled on the grass and blew bubbles too.
What we saw next made us feel bad:
A hippo walked by looking real sad.
"I'm Marty McDinkle, and this is Clyde.
He's my best friend," I added with pride.
"I'm Hippita Hippo, how do you do?"
I asked, "Would you like some iced tea too?"
She thanked me as she took a cup
And in one big gulp drank it all up.
Clyde asked, "What is the matter, my dear?"
As she tried to wipe a face full of tears.
"I see you've been crying," Clyde softly said.
"May I ask what is wrong?
Your eyes are all red."

So Hippita sat and told her sad tale.
"I dream of flying, but I always fail.
And what makes it even harder
Is I'm not too fond of being in water.
That makes all my hippo friends laugh,
I don't even enjoy taking a bath."
"So all the hippos make fun of me;
They say I'm not the way I'm supposed to be.
Then they sing a mean old song
And sing and sing it all day long."

Splishetty, splashetty
Dippity dashetty
What kind of hippo are you?
We all love the water and you should too.
Everyone knows hippos can't fly
So get your big head out of the sky;
Come down in the mud with us
And stop making such a fuss!
Splishetty, splashetty
Dippity dashetty
What kind of hippo are you?
We all love the water and you should, too.

I said, "That's an awful thing they do.
And an awful song they sing to you."
She said, "That's not all. I told a bird.
It wasn't long until all the birds heard.
They crow that I'm much too big to fly
And chirp, Hippos don't belong in the sky.
Then they sing a mean old song
And sing and sing it all day long."

Cheepetty Chirpetty Cawww-petty Hum
Flippetty flappetty, You're so dumb!
We never heard such a silly thing;
Hippos can't fly; you don't have wings.
Quacketty Honketty Squawketty Coo
Your idea's crazy and so are you.

"They said I should stay down in the dirt
And made this hippo's heart really hurt.
But nothing is going to keep me down,
I belong in the sky, not on the ground."

"So I tried real hard to build some wings
I made them out of wood, cloth, and things
And jumped from a high hill nearby
And, for a moment, I was in the sky,
Then my wings broke and I thought I'd crash,
But I hit the lake with a great big splash.
I then bought a ticket for an airplane ride
And walked up the ramp to the plane with pride,
But when I squeezed in the narrow door,
All of a sudden, I crashed through the floor.
So they won't even let me near a plane
And now here I am on the ground again."
Huge hippo tears fell from Hippita's eyes.
But Clyde said, "You're in for a big surprise.
I have a friend that you'll meet real soon
And he has a great big, hot air balloon.
If anyone can help Hippita fly, he can."
So we followed Clyde to meet the man.

When he saw her, he shook his head sadly,

"If you use this balloon, it will end badly."

But Clyde wasn't worried and he used his head.

"What if we build a bigger balloon? he said.

"And build a stronger basket too."

The man smiled and said, "I think that might do."

We began to work as a team right away

So it felt less like work and more like play.

Because we were having so much fun,

Before we knew it, we were done.

Hippita climbed the ramp with a smile so wide

When we all got in, we were filled with pride.

Clyde cranked the hot air burner to high,

Soon the balloon floated in the sky.

But the basket was still on the ground

And then they heard an unusual sound.

The ropes holding the basket began to groan

And the basket itself seemed to moan.

It quivered and shivered and creaked and squeaked.

All that noise gave us quite a big scare,

Then all of a sudden, we were in the air.

Up we floated as the big burner roared;

Higher than the tallest trees we soared.

Clyde and I cheered, "Hippo, Hippo, Hooray!

Hippita Hippo, you've made our day!"

She blushed and smiled as we flew.

Clyde told her, "It's all because of you.

You had a dream you wouldn't let die,

And because of it we ALL can fly!

Then flocks of birds saw Hippita float by,

And she saw the surprise in their eyes.

Herds of hippos in the water below

Saw her fly by with her face all aglow.

"Dear friends," she yelled, "my dream came true

And I believe it can happen for you.

Dare to dream big and do all you can.

I'll cheer you on and be a big fan.

The world needs dreamers who are doers too,

And always remember I'm rooting for you!"

Clyde and Hoozy Whatzadingle

Clyde is a giraffe who is all green
From top to bottom and in-between.
Hoozy Whatzadingle is really quite red
From the tip of his feet to the top of his head.
Though Whatzadingles are usually blue
All have yellow frammoos like Hoozy's hairdo.
Clyde said to his friend who was working away,
"Hello, Hoozy. How's your day?"
Hoozy replied, "I'm slyer than a herd of foxes;
By building my house with cardboard boxes."
Clyde saw bunches of boxes and glue.
He asked, "May I make a suggestion to you?"
But Hoozy frowned and shook his head no
And said, "If you don't mind, would you please go?
I really don't need anyone's help.
I plan to build it all by myself!"
Clyde thought that Hoozy was being quite rude.
There was no need for that attitude.
But, if Hoozy wanted to build it alone,
He had the right to work on his own.

So Clyde left to find friends and play,

But he came back the very next day.

Hoozy said with pride, "My house is done."

But Clyde saw no windows, not a single one.

Clyde started to say, "It's dark inside."

But knew Hoozy was too full of pride.

"I know it's dark," Hoozy said with a scowl.

Now Hoozy's temper was really foul.

"I plan to fix all that tonight.

Come back then to see my light.

But right now, please go away;

I've got more things to do today.

I'll do it all without your help.

Please let me work all by myself."

So Clyde left that boastful guy

And shook his head with a sad, sad sigh.

But, when Clyde returned that night,

He saw a most frightful sight.

His friend was swaying way up high,
Waving a great big spoon in the sky
While standing on a pineapple pie
Balanced on a rickety ladder.
But what made Clyde even sadder
Is beneath it was a great big ball
In an old bathtub, and that wasn't all
Under the tub was a big blue bike
Balanced on a bright red trike
In a wheelbarrow painted white
On a broken bucket. Oh, what a sight!
Hoozy saw Clyde and bellowed down
To the green giraffe on the ground.
"See? I told you I was smart!
I had a plan right from the start."
He pointed to the star-filled sky,
"See all those blinking fireflies?
I'll scoop them up with my wooden spoon
And put them in all my rooms.
There will be a lot of light to see.
No one around is smarter than me."

Clyde saw danger and started to shout,
But Hoozy yelled, "Please just get out!
I'm going to do this all by myself.
I have no need for your help."
Then they heard a great big rumble;
Stuff fell off and started to crumble.
That massive mess began to fall
With poor Hoozy, his pride, and all.
The teetering tower came crashing down
Leaving Hoozy in a heap on the ground.
But still that boastful guy told Clyde,
"I'm going to bed," as he went inside.
In the darkness, he fell deep asleep.
In fact, his sleep was so deep
He didn't hear the pitter-pat
Nor any of the rat-a-tat-tat.
That poor guy didn't hear a sound
As a great rainstorm came pouring down.

Clyde knew that Hoozy was in trouble
So he ran right over on the double.
What he saw was sad indeed;
The poor soaked fellow was a friend in need.
For once, old Hoozy had nothing to say.
His cardboard house had melted away,
Covering him in the muckiest muck.
Hoozy knew then he'd run out of luck.
"I've come to this
    through foolish pride.
I'd like your help now,"
    Hoozy cried.
"I've learned my lesson;
    you'll see I've grown.
No need to be
    all on my own.
We'll have more fun as a team."
Clyde wisely said, "I see what you mean.
Yes, we'll build your house together.
But first, let's wait 'til sunny weather."
The soaked red guy told the green giraffe,
"Great idea!" and they began to laugh.

A Day in the Shade of a Tickletoe Tree

One day in the shade of a Tickletoe Tree,
As Clyde and I slurped Burzleberry Tea
And the tree's leaves swayed in the breeze,
Tickling my toes and Clyde's knobby knees,
We thought how funny the world would be...
If a snail had a tail that curled like a pig's,
And bald eagles liked to wear wigs.
Or if hippos had unicorn horns,
Would they be called Hippocorns?
What if books had no words
But flew around like hummingbirds?
Wouldn't it be neat if whales had feet
And could walk down the street?
What if horseflies were tiny horses
That actually flew?
I don't think it would be fun
To be bitten by one, do you?

What if butter came from butterflies?

That would certainly be a surprise!

Would it be as crazy as it seems

If jelly came from jelly beans?

What if fruit came from animals

And meat grew on trees?

If honey came from cows,

And bees made cheese?

What if ears of corn had thorns and horns?

They'd be hard to eat,

And popcorn wouldn't be a treat!

What if cars rode a bus and buses rode us?

What if boats couldn't float

Unless filled with goats and oats?

What if we were on a carousel horse

That could roam free?

I wonder where he'd take me

And what we would see.

What if everyone walked on their hands

And wore balloons on their feet,

Or sat with their heads right on their seats?

What if everyone looked exactly the same?

How would we ever remember their names?

What if everyone played flutes with their nose

Or strummed guitars with their toes?

What if rainbows made rain or maybe even bows?

They both would be colorful, I suppose.

But what if rainbows were only one color, and it was gray?

I think they'd look mighty boring that way!

All day in the shade of a Tickletoe Tree,

Clyde and I slurp Burzleberry Tea,

And the tree's leaves sway in the breeze,

Tickling my toes and Clyde's knobby knees.

We think how funny the world would be...

The End

About the Author

Russ lives with his wife in Campbell, California. They've been married since 1979 and have three children and three grandsons. In addition to enjoying his family and friends, and his dual passions for investing and writing, Russ loves to spend time in nature, especially near rivers and streams that run through giant redwood groves, and near beautiful beaches. He enjoys watching classic movies, reading, and tending to his small fern garden and redwood grove. Russ manages the investments of the wealth management firm he founded in 2003. He has published fifteen books, nine of which are children's books.

Russ's books can all be found on Amazon. His Amazon Author Page can be found at www.amazon.com/author/russtowne.

Russ's Blog
www.ClydeandFriends.com

Stay updated on Russ's latest children's books, apps, songs, and merchandise (featuring the animated characters that appear in his stories). Readers get sneak previews of special stories, background information about where his story ideas come from and how they are developed, and opportunities to help Russ prioritize the order in which his stories and books should be published, the look, and sometimes the names of some of his characters.

Books for Young Children

V. G. and Dexter Dufflebee

The Grumpadinkles

Ki-Gra's REALLY, REALLY BIG Day!

The Duck Who Flew Upside Down

Clyde and Friends

Clyde and Hoozy Whatzadingle

Clyde and I Help a Hippo to Fly

Rusty Bear and Thomas Too

Clyde and I

Children's App
Based on Characters from the Clyde Books

Clyde and Friends children's app developed by Gail Nelson
using characters from Russ's series of Clyde books:
www.ClydeandFriends.com

www.ingramcontent.com/pod-product-compliance
Lightning Source LLC
Chambersburg PA
CBHW060752150426
42811CB00058B/1386